Nature's Wonders

YELLOWSTONE NATIONAL PARK

Byron Augustin and Jake Kubena

mc Marshall Cavendish
Benchmark
New York

Marshall Cavendish Benchmark
99 White Plains Road
Tarrytown, NY 10591
www.marshallcavendish.us

Expert Reader: Cheryl Jaworowski, Geologist, Yellowstone Center for Resources,
Yellowstone National Park, Wyoming

Library of Congress Cataloging-in-Publication Data
Augustin, Byron.
Yellowstone National Park / by Byron Augustin and Jake Kubena.
p. cm. — (Nature's Wonders)
Includes bibliographical references and index.
Summary: "Provides comprehensive information on the geography, history, wildlife, peoples,
and environmental issues of Yellowstone National Park"—Provided by publisher.
ISBN 978-0-7614-3936-3
1. Yellowstone National Park—Juvenile literature. 2. Natural history—
Yellowstone National Park—Juvenile literature. I. Kubena, Jake, 1982– II. Title.
F722.A93 2010
978.7'52—dc22
2008024555

Editor: Christine Florie
Publisher: Michelle Bisson
Art Director: Anahid Hamparian
Series Designer: Kay Petronio

Photo research by Connie Gardner

Cover photo by Thomas Moran/Corbis
The photographs in this book are used by permission and through the courtesy of:
Art Life Images: All Canada Photos Inc., 4; age footstock, 10, 15; *Corbis:* James Leynse, 18; Tony
Waltham/Robert Harding, 21; W. Perry Conway, 22; Stan Osolinski, 28; Darrell Gulin, 34; Gavriel
Jecan, 39; Kevin Morris, 43; William Henry Jackson, 54; Geoffrey Clements, 55, 63; Thomas Moran,
57; James Amos, 62; Anders Ryman, 66; Historical, 68; Dewitt Jones, 73; Bob Krist, 75; Lake County
Museum, 77; Jeff Vanuga, 78; *Peter Arnold:* Wildlife, 70; *Photo Researchers:* Gregory G. Dimijian, 17; *Art
Resource:* Smithsonian American art Museum, Washington, DC, 47, 60; *Bridgeman Art Library:* Giantess
Geyserin Yellowstone National Park, Reverend Samuel Manning; *Granger:* 52; *The Image Works:* Alinari
Archives, 58; *SuperStock:* Charles Schafer, 24; Mark Newman, 36; age footstock, 38; Tom Benoit, 84;
Minden Pictures: Michael Quinton, 26–27; Mark Rayercroft, 31; Tim Fitzharris, 32; Yva Momatiuk,
35, 40, 89; *Getty Images:* Stephanie Simpson, 8; Richard Bloom, 45; Ted Wood, 81; *North Wind Picture
Archive;* 46; *Alamy:* Lee Foster, 9.

Maps (p. 6 and p. 12) by Mapping Specialists Limited

Printed in Malaysia

135642

CONTENTS

One   A National Treasure   5

Two   The Power of Nature   11

Three   Animals and Plants of Yellowstone   29

Four   Birth of a Concept   47

Five   Changing Cultures   59

Six   A Conflict of Opinions   71

Glossary   88

Fast Facts   89

Find Out More   91

Index   92

ONE

A National Treasure

On March 1, 1872, President Ulysses S. Grant signed a historic document. Known as the Yellowstone National Park Act, the document created the world's first national park. Yellowstone was the first building block in the U.S. National Park Service. Today the National Park Service administers 391 areas. Those areas cover more than 131,000 square miles (339,000 square kilometers) of land.

The creation of Yellowstone marked the first time in history that a country's government recognized that the wilderness belonged to all citizens. This concept of protecting some of a country's natural areas led to an international movement to establish national parks. This preservation movement may have been Yellowstone National Park's greatest impact on the world and its inhabitants.

Yellowstone National Park was created to protect a rare and beautiful national treasure. It covers 3,472 square miles (8,992 sq km) of territory. The park's total area is larger than the combined size of Rhode Island and Delaware. Most of the park—96 percent of it—is located in northwestern Wyoming. There are thin pieces of

Yellowstone National Park offers such a wealth of natural diversity that it truly is a wonder of the world.

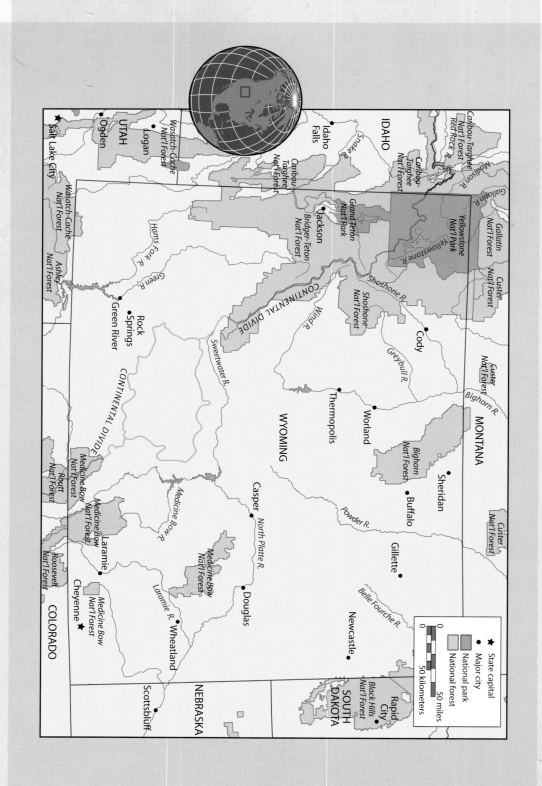

GEOPOLITICAL MAP OF YELLOWSTONE NATIONAL PARK

IDAHO

UTAH

Salt Lake City

Ogden

Logan

Wasatch-Cache Nat'l Forest

Wasatch-Cache Nat'l Forest

Ashley Nat'l Forest

Idaho Falls

Caribou-Targhee Nat'l Forest

Caribou-Targhee Nat'l Forest

Caribou-Targhee Nat'l Forest

Snake R.

Red Rock R.

Madison R.

Gallatin R.

Gallatin Nat'l Forest

Custer Nat'l Forest

MONTANA

Yellowstone Nat'l Park

Yellowstone R.

Grand Teton Nat'l Park

Jackson

Bridger-Teton Nat'l Forest

Shoshone R.

Shoshone Nat'l Forest

Wind R.

CONTINENTAL DIVIDE

Green River

Rock Springs

Hams Fork R.

Green R.

Sweetwater R.

CONTINENTAL DIVIDE

WYOMING

Cody

Greybull R.

Custer Nat'l Forest

Bighorn R.

Thermopolis

Worland

Bighorn Nat'l Forest

Sheridan

Buffalo

Powder R.

Gillette

Casper

North Platte R.

Medicine Bow R.

Medicine Bow Nat'l Forest

Medicine Bow Nat'l Forest

Routt Nat'l Forest

Roosevelt Nat'l Forest

Laramie

Medicine Bow Nat'l Forest

Cheyenne

Laramie R.

Wheatland

Douglas

Belle Fourche R.

Newcastle

COLORADO

Scottsbluff

NEBRASKA

Black Hills Nat'l Forest

SOUTH DAKOTA

Rapid City

★ State capital
● Major city
National park
National forest

0   50 kilometers
0   50 miles

parkland in southwestern Montana (3 percent) and southeastern Idaho (1 percent).

FIRE, ICE, AND QUAKES

Yellowstone has been the site of major geologic activity for millions of years. Massive volcanic eruptions shaped much of the park's surface. The source of those eruptions, a chamber of hot **magma**, is still present and is responsible for the impressive thermal features that are a major tourist attraction. Earthquakes occur almost every day in the park. Sometimes several earthquakes occur during the same day. Most are too small to be felt by humans.

Glaciers scoured the surface between 15,000 and 20,000 years ago. These large ice sheets also helped modify the landscape.

HUMAN ACTIVITY

For more than 12,000 years human groups originally from eastern Asia lived in the area. They were hunters and gatherers who seldom

The Name Game

Yellowstone National Park takes its name from the Yellowstone River, which flows northward from the southern border of the park into Montana. Most historians believe that the river was named by French fur trappers. The trappers translated the American-Indian name Mi tsi a-da-zi for the region to Roche Jaune, or Yellow Stone. The American-Indian name probably arose because of the yellow rock walls in the Grand Canyon of the Yellowstone.

Hot magma lies below the surface of Yellowstone, contributing to its geothermal features. Here, steam rises from hot springs in the park.

stayed long in one location. These groups moved from place to place in search of food obtained by hunting, fishing, and collecting wild edibles. The balance between humans and nature began to change after the Lewis and Clark Expedition. John Colter, a member of the expedition, as well as fur trappers, were the first European Americans to see the natural wonders of Yellowstone. Their stories excited the public and generated interest in this remote wilderness. The intrigue attracted official expeditions whose members returned east with fascinating stories, photographs, and paintings. Soon, proposals were presented to preserve and protect the area. After the official creation of Yellowstone National Park, tourism became a major source of income for the region. Today, nearly 3 million people visit Yellowstone each year.

The work of National Park Service employees is difficult. They have the responsibility of protecting a fragile natural environment. They are also responsible for helping tourists enjoy the rare physical features and wonderful wildlife in the park. Balancing these two goals that often conflict with each other is a major challenge. The dedicated people of the National Park Service strive every day to meet that challenge.

Employees of the National Park Service are responsible for overseeing the protection of the park and its visitors.

Special Sites

National Historic Landmarks are important historic and cultural places. The National Park Service investigates places that are potential landmarks and makes recommendations to the secretary of the interior about which should be recognized. The secretary is the final authority in the selection process. There are about 2,500 U.S. National Historic Landmarks. Yellowstone National Park contains five of them: Fort Yellowstone; the Norris, Madison, and Fishing Bridge Museums; Obsidian Cliff; the Old Faithful Inn; and the Northeast Entrance Station have all been honored with this title.

TWO

The Power of Nature

Most of Yellowstone National Park is located on a high, volcanic plateau. Several creeks and rivers have cut into the plateau's surface. The average elevation of the park is about 8,000 feet (2,438 meters) above sea level. The park has mountains on its northern, eastern, and southern borders. These mountains extend into the park and add to the beauty of the area. The most dominant mountain range is the Absaroka Range. It runs parallel to the eastern boundary of the park. Eagle Peak, at 11,358 feet (3,462 m), is the highest point in Yellowstone.

Many adventurers who have visited Yellowstone comment on what a special place it is. The park has provided moments of peace and harmony with nature for many visitors. However, the natural forces that created Yellowstone were anything but peaceful. Violent volcanic eruptions, powerful earthquakes, and massive glaciers have helped shape the region.

◄ *Yellowstone's landscape formed over the course of thousands of years as a result of volcanic activity, earthquakes, and glaciers. This is the Midway Geyser Basin.*

PHYSICAL MAP OF YELLOWSTONE NATIONAL PARK

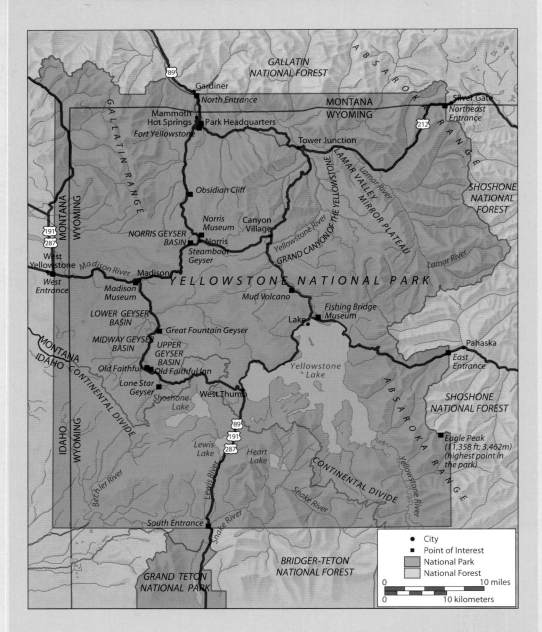

GALLATIN NATIONAL FOREST

ABSAROKA RANGE

89
Gardiner
North Entrance

MONTANA
WYOMING

Silver Gate
Northeast Entrance
212

Mammoth Hot Springs
Park Headquarters
Fort Yellowstone

Tower Junction

GALLATIN RANGE

Obsidian Cliff

Lamar River

MIRROR PLATEAU

LAMAR VALLEY

SHOSHONE NATIONAL FOREST

MONTANA
WYOMING

Norris Museum

Canyon Village

NORRIS GEYSER BASIN

Norris
Steamboat Geyser

GRAND CANYON OF THE YELLOWSTONE

Yellowstone River

Lamar River

191
287

West Yellowstone

West Entrance

Madison River

Madison

YELLOWSTONE NATIONAL PARK

Madison Museum

LOWER GEYSER BASIN

Mud Volcano

Lake

Fishing Bridge Museum

Pahaska

East Entrance

MIDWAY GEYSER BASIN

Great Fountain Geyser

UPPER GEYSER BASIN

Old Faithful
Old Faithful Inn

Lone Star Geyser

Shoshone Lake

West Thumb

Yellowstone Lake

ABSAROKA RANGE

SHOSHONE NATIONAL FOREST

MONTANA
IDAHO
CONTINENTAL DIVIDE

89
191
287

Lewis Lake

Heart Lake

Yellowstone River

Eagle Peak
(11,358 ft; 3,462m)
(highest point in the park)

IDAHO
WYOMING

Bechler River

Lewis River

CONTINENTAL DIVIDE

Snake River

Snake River

South Entrance

BRIDGER-TETON NATIONAL FOREST

GRAND TETON NATIONAL PARK

- • City
- ■ Point of Interest
- National Park
- National Forest

0 _____ 10 miles
0 _____ 10 kilometers

HOT SPOTS

Yellowstone is a hot spot. A hot spot is an area of long-lived **volcanism**. Thermal features and volcanic eruptions are commonly associated with hot spots. In Yellowstone magma lies only 5 miles (8 km) below much of the park's surface.

The partially molten rock underneath Yellowstone is the source of its heat. Scientists have termed the park's magma chamber a supervolcano. Geologic evidence indicates that the Yellowstone supervolcano has erupted catastrophically three times in the past 2 million years.

The last disastrous eruption occurred 640,000 years ago. It was one of the most powerful natural events in the history of the world. A **caldera** measuring 28 miles (45 km) wide and 47 miles (76 km) long was created when the volcano exploded with amazing force. More than 240 cubic miles (1,000 cubic km) of rock, lava, and ash, along with scorching hot gas, rocketed into the atmosphere. Some of the ash circled the globe for days, perhaps weeks. This event likely affected the earth's climate.

Along the rim of the caldera, liquid ash flowed outward at a speed of more than 100 miles per hour (161 km per hour). In a puff of steam and hot ash all living things in the ash flow's path were quickly destroyed. In a matter of a few hours or at most a few days, the eruption ended. An entire **ecosystem** was erased from the face of the earth. The landscape that we recognize as Yellowstone today was lifeless and barren.

Today, the supervolcano is resting, but it is still very much alive. It continues to supply the heat producing the geothermal features that help make the park famous.

GEOTHERMAL ACTIVITY

Nature has created a complex network of underground plumbing that allows heated water to reach the surface. At the surface, thermal waters form features such as hot springs, fumaroles, mud pots, and geysers. Yellowstone contains more than ten thousand individual geothermal features. These features account for more than half of all the geothermal features on Earth.

Hot springs are the most common geothermal feature in Yellowstone. They are created when heated underground water rises, creating pools of hot water on the earth's surface. The water in many hot springs is hotter than 150 degrees Fahrenheit (66 degrees Celsius). In the hottest springs the temperature may

When heated underground water ▶▶
rises to the surface, it creates hot
springs, which are quite common
throughout Yellowstone.

exceed 205 °F (96 °C). Hot springs can be very dangerous. Visitors to the park should always be cautious around the scalding hot water. During the park's history more than one hundred visitors have been badly burned. At least nineteen people have died when they accidentally fell into or carelessly entered the springs.

Fumaroles are steam vents in the earth's surface. The water boiling underground generates steam that rises to the surface and exits through small holes in the ground, often making a hissing noise that can be heard from a great distance. The steam may contain **hydrogen sulfide** gas, which makes the air smell like rotten eggs.

Mud pots resemble bubbling pools of paint. In fact, some mud pots are called paint pots. **Sulfuric acid** helps dissolve the surrounding rock into clay mixed with water. During dry periods the mud pots are especially thick with dissolved minerals. After rains the mud pots become diluted with water and have a much thinner consistency. Hydrogen sulfide surrounding the mud pots may infuse the air with an unpleasant odor.

A geyser is a hot spring that periodically sprays water and steam above the ground. In order to erupt, geysers require heat, water, and a plumbing system. The heat is provided by Yellowstone's magma chamber. Snowmelt and rain supply the water. The cracks in the rocks form the natural plumbing system underground.

Geysers erupt when water is heated underground in a natural plumbing system. Eventually, the water becomes so hot that it flashes to steam, causing an eruption. After the hot water and steam

These tiny fumaroles, at only 2 inches (7 centimeters) across, are found at Yellowstone's Mammoth Springs.

have been expelled, the underground plumbing system begins to refill with cool water. This sets the stage for the heating of water and the next eruption.

The most famous geyser in Yellowstone is Old Faithful, named by the Washburn-Doane Expedition in 1870 because of the frequency and regularity of its eruptions. Over the years the frequency and length of the geyser's eruptions have changed, but they are still predictable. The eruptions shoot water an average of 130 feet (40 m) into the air. They last about a minute and a half.

The most well-known geyser in Yellowstone National Park is Old Faithful, whose eruptions reach heights of 130 feet (40 m).

Steamboat Geyser

Although it is not as well known as Old Faithful, Steamboat Geyser is very special. It has the highest eruption of any geyser in the world. During its most powerful eruptions, water and steam can spray more than 300 feet (91 m) into the air. The geyser is highly unpredictable, with long periods of time between eruptions.

SHAKING UP YELLOWSTONE

Yellowstone National Park's earthquakes are evidence of its active volcanism. Scientists monitor earthquakes by using an instrument called a seismograph. It detects how much motion in the earth's crust takes place during an earthquake. The amount of motion is recorded on a numerical scale known as the Richter scale. The Richter scale begins at zero and usually rates earthquakes from a scale of one to nine, though the scale's ratings are limitless.

There have been six earthquakes in the park that registered above 6.0 but none above 7.0. Between one and twenty earthquakes are recorded on most days in Yellowstone. Almost all of these events have measurements below 3.0. At that level of intensity, most park visitors do not even notice them.

Most of the earthquakes in Yellowstone are caused by the movement of fluids and gases through cracks in the rocks below the surface. The most activity is found near the northwest corner of the ancient caldera. This caldera is located near the park's center. Large, intense earthquakes can produce surface cracks, new fumaroles, and the appearance of cloudy water in the hot springs. Earthquakes can occasionally cause changes in the timing and regularity of some geyser eruptions.

The most interesting characteristic of Yellowstone's earthquakes is that several of them often occur in a short amount of time. These events are referred to as **swarms**. In April of 2004 more than four hundred separate earthquakes were recorded during a period of three days. Other major swarms were observed in 1973, 1985, and 1995.

THE BIG CHILL

During the last Ice Age a giant ice cap 3,100 to 4,000 feet (945 to 1,219 m) thick covered most of the park. The tops of some of the highest peaks in the Absaroka Range were barely visible.

The glaciers contributed to reshaping the surface of the park. The weight of the ice on the surface scoured and gouged out formations in some areas, and meltwater deposited soil and rock in others. About 14,000 years ago, when the last major Ice Age ended, meltwater running out of the glaciers helped produce some of today's drainage patterns. The glaciers also helped create some of the park's majestic waterfalls. There are more than three hundred in Yellowstone

One of the most dramatic waterfalls in Yellowstone is the Lower Falls.

National Park. The park has the highest density of waterfalls of any region in the world. The Upper and Lower Falls on the Yellowstone River are magnificent. Water tumbles over the Upper Falls for 109 feet (33 m) and over the Lower Falls for 308 feet (94 m).

Two Directions

Yellowstone National Park is located on the **continental divide**. The water from its streams eventually flows into two different oceans. The Yellowstone River flows north and east to the Missouri River. The Missouri continues a long journey to the Mississippi River and on to the Gulf of Mexico, a part of the Atlantic Ocean. In the southwest corner of the park the Bechler and Lewis rivers dump their waters into the Snake River. The Snake River then joins the Columbia River before discharging into the Pacific Ocean.

The Yellowstone River is the major river system in the park. Its source is in the Absaroka Mountains, just outside the park's southern boundary. The river flows gently into Lake Yellowstone. As it exits the lake, the river begins the remainder of its 670-mile (1,078-km) trip to meet the Missouri River. Shortly after flowing out of the northern edge of Yellowstone Lake, the river passes violently over three waterfalls. In this portion of its path the river has carved out the magnificent Grand Canyon of the Yellowstone. The canyon is 24 miles (39 km) long, with depths from 800 to 1,200 feet (244 to 366 m). The rock walls of the canyon display some of the most brilliant colors in the park. The Yellowstone is the longest river in the lower forty-eight states that does not have a dam across its course.

◄ *The Yellowstone River flows through the deep, golden-colored Grand Canyon of the Yellowstone in Yellowstone National Park.*

Yellowstone Lake

The largest water feature found in the park is Yellowstone Lake. It covers 132 square miles (342 sq km). The lake has 141 miles (227 km) of shoreline. The average depth of the water is 140 feet (43 m). Its greatest depth, however, is almost 400 feet (122 m) below the surface of the lake. It is the country's largest freshwater lake that is above 7,000 feet (2,134 m) in elevation. Approximately half of the lake is located in the ancient volcanic caldera formed almost 640,000 years ago. The lake is a favorite fishing destination for park visitors. It has the highest concentration of native cutthroat trout of any lake in the United States.

THE CLIMATE FACTOR

Yellowstone's climate is strongly impacted by its elevation and its location on the eastern side of the Rocky Mountains. This elevation keeps daily temperatures cool. During the summer months the park can be warm and pleasant during the day. At night it frequently cools to 40 °F (4.4 °C). Winters in Yellowstone can be harsh. Cold Arctic air from Canada enters the park on a regular basis. Daytime winter temperatures can hover around 0 °F (−17.8 °C). The nighttime temperature may fall to −50 °F (−45.6 °C).

The Rocky Mountains block much of the moisture carried from the Pacific Ocean into the continent. This mountain range creates a semiarid climate in the park, which receives 15 to 20 inches (381 to 508 millimeters) of precipitation annually. May and June are typically the wettest months, although precipitation levels do not vary much throughout the year. Snow usually begins to fall in late October and lasts into April. Most of the park's roads are closed to wheeled vehicles in the winter season, as they are groomed and plowed for winter recreation.

The four seasons experienced in Yellowstone are very different. Each one has special characteristics that attract tourists. Summer brings the greatest number of visitors. Pleasant temperatures allow tourists to comfortably hike, fish, observe wildlife, and tour the thermal features. In the fall the aspen and other broadleaf trees display beautiful colors. Winter is a bitter season but a wonderful time

to view the geysers. When a geyser erupts, the droplets of steam hang suspended in the heavy, cold winter air. The brilliant white color of the steam against the background of deep blue sky creates a lasting memory. Spring is the season of renewal in the park. It is a perfect time to view wildflowers and baby animals.

Yellowstone's winters are frigid. Here, pools steam in the cold winter air at Mammoth Springs.

THREE

Animals and Plants of Yellowstone

Yellowstone is a park and an ecosystem—a community of animals and plants living together in a particular environment. The legal boundaries of Yellowstone National Park enclose 3,472 square miles (8,992 sq km) that have never been fenced. It is a special place where plants and animals are carefully protected.

The Greater Yellowstone Ecosystem is composed of Yellowstone National Park and Grand Teton National Park. It also includes several national forests, wildlife refuges, private land, and tribal land. Some animals would not be able to survive if they were confined to Yellowstone National Park alone. To be truly free, they must be able to move between the park and these surrounding areas. However, these animals' movements can create problems between government agencies and private landowners.

◄ *An elk surveys its surroundings at Minerva Springs in Yellowstone National Park.*

NATURE'S ZOO

Yellowstone National Park is America's most popular place to view wild animals. Examples of every vertebrate animal living in the park when European Americans arrived are still present. The park is their home.

FLASHING HOOVES

There are seven native species of **ungulates** that live in Yellowstone. These include elk, bison, American pronghorn, moose, bighorn sheep, mule deer, and white-tailed deer. All of these animals were important sources of food for American Indians.

What Is for Dinner?

The animals of Yellowstone eat many different foods. If they eat only the meat of other animals, they are called carnivores. Wolves and coyotes are examples of carnivores. Elk, moose, deer, and beavers are called herbivores because they eat only plants. Some animals, like bears, are omnivores. They eat both plants and other animals.

Yellowstone National Park is home to the world's largest elk population.

Yellowstone has the greatest concentration of elk in the world. During the summer as many as 30,000 elk graze on park meadows. Adult elk weigh between 500 and 700 pounds (227 and 318 kilograms). Mature males (bulls) sometimes weigh half a ton (454 kg). The elk run in herds and communicate with each other using squeaks, barks, whistles, and grunts. During the mating season the bulls bugle, making a high-pitched sound to attract females. The bugle is also used to warn other males to stay away from a bull's harem (group of females). Elk are the favorite food of wolves and coyotes.

The wild bison herd of Yellowstone is descended from the only herd in the world that has survived since prehistoric times. During the early 1800s, 30 to 60 million bison roamed across North America. Most of them were killed for their hides in the 1870s and 1880s. At one point the species was almost extinct, with fewer than one thousand individuals surviving.

Bison, which are sometimes called buffalo, are the largest native mammals in North America. A mature bull can weigh a ton (907 kg).

Bison graze near the steaming vents of Yellowstone.

Bison are very fast for such large animals. In fact, their speed and size make them the most dangerous animals in the park. They can be unpredictable and aggressive. Some tourists who have gotten too close have suffered injuries.

The American pronghorn is often called an antelope. However, it is the only surviving member of an otherwise extinct family of goat-antelopes. The pronghorn is the fastest land animal in the Western Hemisphere and the second fastest in the world, after the cheetah. A pronghorn can run for several miles at a steady speed of 45 miles per hour (72 km per hour). If extra speed is needed to escape a predator, the animal is capable of bursts reaching 60 miles per hour (97 km per hour). A pronghorn can easily outrun a wolf or a coyote.

Moose are the largest members of the deer family. Adult males may weigh 1,500 pounds (680 kg). The males also have large antlers, with a spread of 5 to 6 feet (1.5 to 1.8 m). They use their antlers to attract females and for defense. The males do not help care for young calves and usually live alone. Moose feed mostly on aquatic plants and live near rivers and lakes. They are excellent swimmers and do not fear the water. A moose can hold its breath for thirty seconds and will dive 18 feet (5 m) to reach plants.

Bighorn sheep live on high, craggy slopes in Yellowstone. They have large, curved horns that may weigh 30 to 40 pounds (14 to 18 kg). Bighorn sheep are well known for fighting to prove dominance over other sheep. During a fight they may butt heads at speeds of 20 miles per hour (32 km per hour). The collision of

Yellowstone's rugged hills are home to the area's bighorn sheep.

two large rams produces an explosive sound that echoes across the mountain slopes. These sheep were important in the diet of the Shoshone Indians (also called Sheep Eaters) who lived in Yellowstone.

THE HUNTERS

Nature can sometimes seem cruel. If the populations of certain animals become too large, some individuals may die of disease or starvation. Natural predators help keep populations in check. In the park there are many predators. They include wolves, coyotes, red fox, badgers, river otters, eagles, and hawks.

Wolves are at the top of the predator list. They are the most efficient hunters in the park. They can grow to be more than 6 feet (1.8 m) in length and 3 feet (1 m) in height. Adults often weigh more than 100 pounds (45 kg). Females usually give birth to about five pups. Both males and females share the responsibility of raising the pups.

Wolves are social creatures that live in packs. There are male and female pack leaders that the rest of the pack obeys. Individual packs hunt together and share their kill. By hunting as a team, they can successfully bring down animals ten to fifteen times larger than themselves. Yellowstone is the best place on Earth to observe wolves in the wild.

Yellowstone's most aggressive predator is the wolf.

River otters are the master predators of the aquatic environment. They are members of the weasel family. Their muscular, streamlined bodies and webbed feet make them powerful swimmers. They possess special eyelids that improve their underwater vision. Long facial whiskers help otters sense vibrations in the water and locate prey. Their diet consists of fish, frogs, turtles, muskrats, and young beavers.

Small animals and fish are threatened daily by attacks from the sky. A wide variety of predatory birds are found throughout the park. Eagles, hawks, ospreys, owls, falcons, and kestrels all are efficient hunters. A shadow overhead can mean death for chipmunks, mice, moles, ground squirrels, and fish.

The bald eagle is one of the most respected and loved birds in America. It is the national bird of the United States and a symbol of freedom and liberty. Bald eagles were almost hunted to extinction. However, strict conservation laws have allowed this species to recover.

Mature bald eagles can be 3 feet (1 m) tall and have a wingspan of 6 to 8 feet (1.8 to 2.4 m). They develop a distinctive crown of white feathers on their heads. Their favorite food is fish. They will also

The most majestic bird in Yellowstone is the bald eagle.

eat waterfowl and the meat of animals killed by other predators. For hunting purposes, bald eagles like to roost and nest in the tops of tall trees growing near water.

Eagles mate for life and build their nest together. The nests are massive constructions that can weigh 2 to 2.5 tons (1.8 to 2.3 metric tons). The same nest is used by the pair year after year. Each year the female lays two eggs in March or April that hatch in May. The young eagles have large appetites. Their parents hunt all day to satisfy their demands for food.

OTHER FEATHERED FRIENDS

Bird-watchers have documented at least 318 species of birds in the park, including predatory birds. Some of the other birds that call Yellowstone home are trumpeter swans, sandhill cranes, wild turkeys, great blue herons, and mockingbirds.

The trumpeter swan is an elegant, all-white bird with a black bill and feet. It has a long, graceful neck. It is the largest native waterfowl in North America. An adult swan can stand 4 feet (1.2 m) tall, have an 8-foot (2.4-m) wingspan, and weigh up to 40 pounds (18 kg). It can fly at speeds between 40 and 80 miles per hour (64 and 129 km per hour). The trumpeter swan has a unique call that sounds like a blaring trumpet.

Sandhill cranes can be identified by the red patch on the crowns of their heads. Their long legs are adapted to wading in shallow water and walking on land. Cranes live around marshes and feed

Summer visitors to Yellowstone are sandhill cranes.

on insects, small rodents, and amphibians. They have a distinctive rattling call that can be heard from far away. Sandhill cranes are migratory birds that are usually found in Yellowstone only during the summer. In winter they migrate to the Rio Grande Valley, on the Texas-Mexico border.

Sandhill cranes mate for life and are often seen with their partners throughout the summer. Sandhill cranes are enthusiastic dancers. While courting, both males and females throw their heads into the sky. They call out while high-stepping and jumping up and down with outstretched wings.

THE PARK FAVORITE

Park surveys indicate that bears are the animals that visitors most want to see. Both black bears and grizzly (brown) bears inhabit Yellowstone. They eat both plants and animals, but most of their diet consists of plants. They eat grass, leaves, roots, berries, nuts, seeds, and wild fruit. They also eat insects, fish, and animals.

BUSY AS A BEAVER

Beavers are one of the important animals that attracted the first European

The animal that most visitors hope to see is the bear.

A Long Nap

Both black bears and grizzly bears enter dens during Yellowstone's frigid winters, yet they are not true hibernators. They do, however, fall into a deep sleep for long periods of time. Their body temperature drops four to five degrees, and their pulse slows from forty beats to eight or twelve beats per minute.

To prepare for this long period of inactivity, bears stuff themselves for four to seven months. Some large bears eat 90 pounds (41 kg) of food a day. During this time their weight may double, most of which is fat. This fat is their energy source while they sleep through the long winter season.

Americans to the park region. Beaver pelts (hides) commanded a good price in the eastern United States and in Europe because they were used in popular fashions of the time.

Beavers are the world's second largest rodents, after the South American capybara. They are also expert engineers. They cut trees with their sharp teeth to build dams and lodges to live in. Sometimes they change the environment by blocking streams and creating large ponds. Beavers are excellent swimmers and can stay underwater

A beaver carries a newly cut branch to its dam.

for up to fifteen minutes. Their diets consist mostly of bark, roots, twigs, and aquatic plants.

SNAKES AND LIZARDS

Due to the cold climate Yellowstone has only six species of reptiles. Five of these species are snakes, and one is a lizard.

The wandering garter snake, usually found near water sources, is the most common reptile in Yellowstone. Like a skunk, if it feels threatened, the garter snake can release an unpleasant-smelling chemical.

The prairie rattlesnake is the only poisonous snake in the park. It is brownish colored, with darker oval patterns on its back. It can grow to be 5 feet (1.5 m) in length and has a triangular-shaped head. Its most distinctive feature is the rattle at the end of its tail. The rattle is used to warn intruders that invade its habitat. Prairie rattlesnakes prefer to be left alone.

The sagebrush lizard grows to be about 5 inches (12.7 centimeters) in length. The males have bright blue patches on their bellies, which they use to attract females. Snakes and predatory birds eagerly hunt sagebrush lizards. When a predator tries to grab a lizard's tail, the tail separates from its body. This sometimes confuses the predator and allows the lizard to escape. The lizard's new tail will grow in a few weeks.

THE PERFECT COMBINATION

Yellowstone Park's elevation varies dramatically, ranging from 5,282 feet (1,610 m) to 11,358 feet (3,462 m) above sea level. As the elevation changes, so do the plants.

The vegetation is a mixture of plants, each of which plays a role in the ecology of the park. There are trees, shrubs, vines, grasses, wildflowers, mosses, lichens, and aquatic plants. The plants provide homes, food, and protection for the ecosystem's animals. Eighty percent of the park is forested. At lower elevations cottonwood and willow trees line the stream and river valleys. Higher on the mountain slopes Douglas fir is common. At the highest elevations trees disappear, and alpine meadows dominate. The most common tree species in the park is the lodgepole pine. This species comprises 75 to 80 percent of all the trees in the park. Lodgepole pines grow tall and straight. They were used in the construction of many of the park's historic buildings.

Grasslands carpet 15 percent of the park's surface. The largest grassland meadows are found at

Lodgepole pines border a marshy ▶▶
meadow in Yellowstone National Park.

the lowest elevations. These are located in the northern portion of the park. Two of the most beautiful meadows are in the Hayden and Lamar valleys. The Lamar Valley also contains one of the world's largest petrified forests. The lush, nutritious grasses make these valleys favorite locations for large herds of elk and bison to graze. The meadows also produce a variety of wildflowers that are popular with photographers. The remaining 5 percent of the park is covered with water.

DANGEROUS PLANTS

Plants are seldom thought of as potential killers of humans, but they can be. Several plant species in the park contain poisons that can

Rare Plants

Two plants that grow in Yellowstone National Park are not found anywhere else in the world. Ross's bentgrass thrives in the geyser basins along the Firehole River. It is one of the first grasses to turn green in spring, so it provides early food for grazing animals. Yellowstone sand verbena grows along the shoreline of Yellowstone Lake. It grows much farther north than other species in its family. Thermal activity probably helps this plant survive at the higher latitudes of the park.

make people sick. Others may be deadly if eaten. At least six mushrooms in the park contain poisons capable of causing death.

According to botanists the two most deadly plants in the park are the death camas and water hemlock. Three people have died from eating water hemlock while in the park. They were fooled because water hemlock plants look like wild carrots and wild parsnips. Water hemlock contains a strong toxin that attacks the central nervous system. Ingesting this toxin results in horrible stomach pain and convulsions.

Death camas, a toxic plant, grows in Yellowstone and must not be eaten by visitors.

A good rule to follow when visiting the park is not to touch the plants and animals. Remember, do not leave anything but footprints, and take only photos on a visit to Yellowstone.

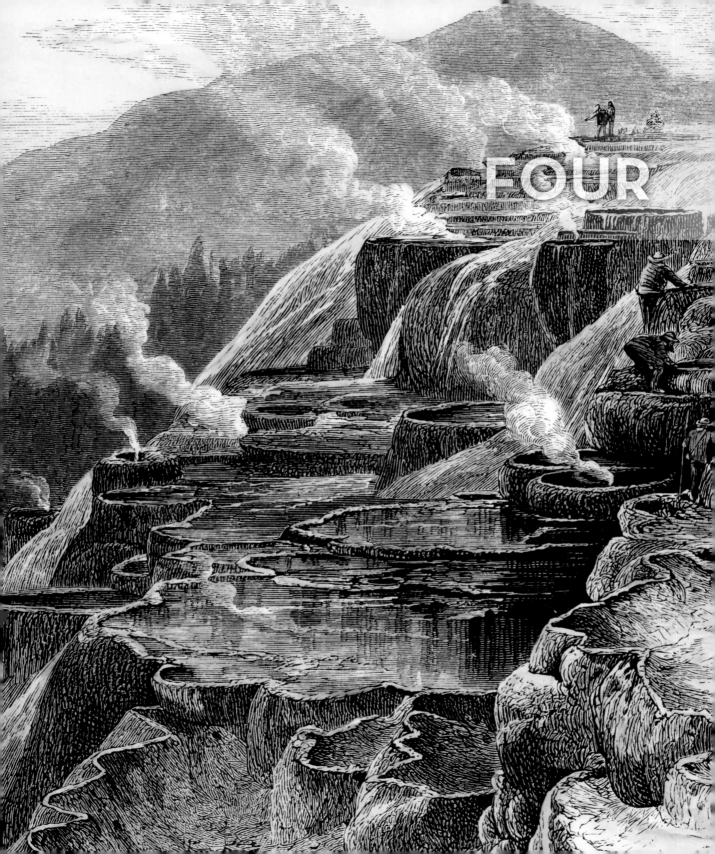

FOUR

Birth of a Concept

Humans have been passing through or living in the Yellowstone area for more than 12,000 years. The first groups of people migrated from Siberia, crossing the narrow land bridge that once connected Asia to North America. These ancient immigrants became the ancestors of several American-Indian tribes that have had a presence in the Yellowstone region.

American Indians began living permanently in the Yellowstone area about three thousand years ago. They hunted bison, deer, elk, and small animals. The park's plants were gathered for food and medicinal uses. American Indians shaped obsidian, a shiny, usually black volcanic rock from the region, into tools and

The Kiowa were an early native tribe who made the Yellowstone region their home from 1400 to 1700.

◄ *Early explorers discover the wonders of Yellowstone National Park.*

weapons. In addition, some geothermal features in the region were used as religious and ceremonial sites.

EARLY EXPLORATION

Historians consider John Colter to be the first European American to explore Yellowstone. Colter was a member of the Lewis and Clark Expedition from 1804 to 1806. On the journey home he decided to stay in the area to try his luck at fur trapping. During the winter of 1807–1808 he traveled alone through much of what is now Yellowstone National Park. Colter kept in touch with William Clark through letters. Colter described gushing geysers and stinking sulfurous springs. William Clark used these descriptions to revise a map he made of unknown features in the territory.

Oral History

Both the Kiowa and Crow Indians have oral histories that involve the Yellowstone region. The Kiowa believe that their creator gave them Yellowstone for their homeland. Archaeological evidence supports the presence of the Kiowa in the area from the 1400s to the 1700s. Later the Kiowa migrated southeast, into what is now Kansas and Oklahoma.

The Crow Indians have preserved a legendary story about the Dragon's Mouth, a geothermal feature in the park. According to their legend a dangerous bison bull was eating their people. A heroic young warrior used magic to change the bull into the Dragon's Mouth. When the feature erupts, the blasts of hot air and steam represent the snorts of the angry bull.

The Great Escape

In 1808 John Colter and his trapping partner John Potts were checking their beaver traps on a small stream in the park. Suddenly they were surrounded by Blackfoot warriors. Potts was killed when the Blackfoot tried to take his rifle. Colter was stripped naked and offered the chance to run for his life.

Colter was given a few hundred yards' head start. He ran straight for the Jefferson River, located 6 miles (9.6 km) away. He was forced to run through cactus in his bare feet. At one point he turned to look over his shoulder and saw that he had far outrun all but one warrior. This warrior was carrying a spear and was gaining ground fast. Colter suddenly stopped. The exhausted and surprised Blackfoot warrior stumbled. He fell to the ground, breaking his spear. Colter picked up a section of the spear and pinned the warrior to the ground, killing him.

Colter once again headed for the river, with the rest of the Blackfoot in hot pursuit. He dove into the river and swam under a large pile of brush. The Indians searched until dark and then gave up. In the darkness of night Colter left his hiding place. He drifted silently with the current miles downstream. A week later he stumbled into a trading post naked, sunburned, and hungry but alive.

Fur trappers related their experiences in Yellowstone, which in turn attracted others to explore the region for themselves.

Other fur trappers followed Colter into present-day Yellowstone. The trappers were great storytellers. Soon their descriptions of the wonders of Yellowstone had reached the eastern states. One of the first written descriptions of the region was published in a Philadelphia newspaper in 1827. The letter from Daniel Potts, a fur trapper, stated, "On the south border of this [Yellowstone] lake is a number of hot and boiling springs some of water and others of most beautiful fine clay and resembles that of a mush pot and throws its particles to the immense height of from twenty to thirty feet [6 to 9 m]."

By the 1840s trapping had greatly reduced the number of beavers and other animals in the park, making the work less profitable. The trappers headed for new, more promising territory. Yellowstone's short fur-trapping era thus came to an end.

THE FOLSOM PARTY

One of the earliest expeditions into Yellowstone was conducted by the Folsom Party in 1869. The group was made up of three friends: William Peterson, Charles Cook, and David Folsom. Peterson had been waiting in Helena, Montana, for an official group to explore the upper waters of the Yellowstone River. However, the formation of this group never occurred. Disappointed, Peterson told his friends Cook and Folsom "that if he could find one companion, he would still like to explore the upper Yellowstone River." Cook and Folsom both agreed to join him. They were the first group to successfully explore much of today's park.

After the Folsom Party returned to Montana, a friend of Cook's encouraged him to publish an account of his adventure. Cook and Folsom combined the diaries they had kept on their journey. They submitted a manuscript to a Chicago-based publication called *Western Monthly Magazine.* The editor omitted parts of the diary and credited only Cook with the writing. Later, in 1894, Nathaniel P. Langford reprinted the combined diaries and credited only Folsom. Langford played a vital role in the eventual creation of Yellowstone National Park. He drew much of his desire to form a park from the accounts of Cook and Folsom.

THE WASHBURN-DOANE EXPEDITION

In 1870 General Henry D. Washburn, cavalry officer Lieutenant Gustavus C. Doane, and Nathaniel P. Langford organized an

Henry D. Washburn was a member of an expedition to Yellowstone in the early 1870s.

expedition to explore and map the Yellowstone region. They discovered that the fantastic stories told by members of past expeditions were true. They explored the geysers, hot pools, waterfalls, flora, and fauna. The party discussed the idea of dividing the region amongst themselves for personal gain, though upon the advice of Montana lawyer Cornelius Hodges, they decided to leave the area for all to enjoy. This was the birth of the concept of a national park.

This was the first expedition to Yellowstone that was supported by the government. The group brought compasses, a thermometer, and an **aneroid barometer**. They carried out their exploration and research of the area for over a month.

THE HAYDEN AND BARLOW PARTIES

After returning from the Washburn-Doane Expedition, Langford began a lecture tour. His audiences included powerful politicians, business leaders, scientists, teachers, and other interested citizens. He described the group's discoveries and encouraged the creation of a national park to protect the region. Ferdinand V. Hayden, the head of the U.S. Geological Survey of the Territories, attended one of his

Lost!

A member of the Washburn-Doane Party, Truman C. Everts, was separated from the expedition on September 9, 1870. After he left his horse untied, it ran off with all of his supplies, including blankets, guns, and matches. He was left on foot with no clue as to the location of the rest of the group. His friends tried to signal him by firing gunshots into the air. They started fires to send up smoke signals. However, Everts had wandered off in the wrong direction and remained lost.

The fact that he survived thirty-seven days in the wilderness was a miracle. He found a magnifying lens in his pocket. He used the lens to focus sunlight on dried leaves to start fires that kept him warm at night. He also found a wild thistle whose root could be eaten. The thistle root was the only food he could find.

As the days passed, he became disoriented and depressed. Then he lost the magnifying lens and began to give up hope. Some of his companions did not give up, however. They made two separate attempts to find him. Finally, they were successful when John Baronett and George Pritchett, two experienced mountain men they had hired, found him on the thirty-seventh day of his ordeal. He was near death and weighed less than 75 pounds (34 kg). He was carried back to civilization and began a slow recovery.

The stories of his disappearance and rescue were published across the country. Everts wrote an article titled "Thirty-Seven Days of Peril" for *Scribner's Monthly*. His story of survival created new interest in and excitement about Yellowstone.

Members of the Hayden expedition make their way past a lake in Yellowstone. This expedition led major geological and geographical surveys of the area.

lectures. Hayden was inspired by Langford's descriptions. He asked the federal government to allow him to lead a new expedition.

The purpose of Hayden's expedition was to collect the most accurate information about Yellowstone yet gathered. Hayden was instructed to map the region. He was also told to collect data about its geology, flora and fauna, and agricultural potential. His team included artists, photographers, a meteorologist, a topographer, a mineralogist, and botanists. Captain John Barlow, the chief engineer of the army's Division of Missouri, also joined the expedition. Although Hayden and Barlow explored the region at the same time, the two groups mostly kept to their own separate work. The expedition produced a massive amount of information. The new information was used to help persuade Congress to set aside a large section of unique land as the world's first national park.

Father of National Parks

Thomas Moran has been credited by many to be the father of national parks. He was the artist hired by *Scribner's Monthly* to illustrate a description of Yellowstone written by Nathaniel P. Langford in 1870. While a member of the Hayden and Barlow parties, Moran drew several sketches of the natural features in the region. When he returned home, he began a series of oil paintings based on those sketches. His most famous painting is *The Grand Canyon of the Yellowstone* (below). The painting was used by the Northern Pacific Railroad to generate publicity after the new national park opened. For years, this painting hung in the Senate lobby of the U.S. Capitol. Currently, it is displayed at the Smithsonian American Art Museum, in Washington, D.C.

The Birth of a Park

After the return of the Hayden and Barlow parties, a national movement to set aside Yellowstone as protected land began in earnest. Hayden recommended in his official report that Yellowstone be protected. Several magazine and newspaper articles also fascinated the public with descriptions of the area's natural wonders and supported the concept of establishing a protected area.

Up for Grabs

As general interest in protecting Yellowstone grew, various groups argued about who should manage the area. The Montana and Wyoming territories both wanted to manage the proposed park. Eventually, the federal government argued that it was not proper for a single territory to manage such a remarkable area. The U.S. Congress took notice. In December 1871 a bill was introduced in Congress to set aside Yellowstone for federal management.

The approval of the bill was greatly aided by the testimonies of Hayden and Langford. Hayden illustrated his testimony with numerous items he brought back from Yellowstone. He possessed the skills and credibility to describe the unique geography and geology of the area. In addition, the stunning photos taken by William Jackson had a positive influence on the decision. Hayden concluded his testimony by declaring that Yellowstone was without agricultural, mineral, or manufacturing value. In his opinion the area would best be used for scientific research and public recreation.

The Northern Pacific Railroad

The Northern Pacific Railroad also played a role in the creation of Yellowstone National Park. The railroad recognized the potential for tourism and established plans to build a rail line to the park's northern entrance. If they could help convince Congress to create a park, they could make money selling train tickets to eastern tourists.

Jay Cooke, a financier of the Northern Pacific Railroad, was influential in promoting the park. Cooke financed Nathaniel Langford's lectures and secured Thomas Moran's place in the Hayden Expedition. Cooke also had many important friends in Congress, whom he quietly persuaded to support the legislation. After some debate in Congress, the bill to create Yellowstone National Park was passed by both the House and the Senate. On March 1, 1872, President Ulysses S. Grant signed the Yellowstone National Park Act into law. On this historic date the country's and the world's first national park was born. This poster (right), used by the Northern Pacific Railroad, is based on Thomas Moran's famous Yellowstone painting.

 YELLOWSTONE PARK

FIVE

Changing Cultures

Anthropologists believe the first humans to enter present-day Yellowstone National Park came from Asia. Gradually, they migrated southward from Alaska and arrived in the Yellowstone region more than 12,000 years ago. The American Indians present when the European Americans arrived are believed to be descendants of those early Asiatic peoples.

American Indians used the Yellowstone area for thousands of years without causing much environmental damage. They lived in harmony with the environment and respected all living things. They did not think of themselves as superior to other animals. Killing animals for food was necessary for survival. Killing more than they could use was considered wasteful and wrong.

No one owned the land. Because the American Indians were frequently on the move, having wealth in the form of material items was not important to them. Tribal leaders carefully watched the supply of wood for fires and the number of edible plants and animals in an area. When they thought they had harvested enough of an area's

◄ *Shoshone Indians were a tribe who made Yellowstone their home before it was a national park.*

American Indians in the Yellowstone region met their needs by using only the natural resources they needed. This illustration depicts them drying meat and dressing robes.

resources, they moved to a new location. After their departure, the earth would have time to heal.

Family and tribal groups varied in size. Men were the leaders and decision makers. Usually a respected elder was the tribal leader or chief. He almost always met with a tribal council before making important decisions.

Males were responsible for hunting and for training their older sons in the ways of the tribe. Women held the responsibility of raising the children, cooking, and gathering wild berries, nuts, and seeds. They made and repaired clothing for their families. Children were expected to do chores. Boys learned to hunt at an early age.

Girls frequently helped care for younger children. Girls observed their mothers and learned how to be good wives. All children were taught to treat their elders with respect.

Organized religion was not a part of their lives. However, the American Indians who lived in the area were spiritual people. They believed in a creator and worshiped many things in the natural environment. Storytellers shared ancient beliefs and group history around campfires. Because these groups did not have a written language, this storytelling was essential for passing information and beliefs to younger generations.

The Beginning

Most American Indians believed in a creator who was responsible for making the earth. The Blackfoot called the creator Napi, or Old Man. The following is one example of an Indian creation story:

In the beginning all the world was water. One day Old Man, either by design or because he was just curious, decided to find out what might lie beneath the water. He sent animals to dive below the surface. . . . At last muskrat rose slowly to the surface, holding between his paws a little ball of mud. Old Man took this small lump of mud and blew upon it. The mud began to swell. It continued to grow larger until it became the whole earth.

—Blackfoot Creation Story by Jim Kipp, http://trailtribes.org

Twenty-six American-Indian groups have lived in what is now the park, including the Sioux, Comanche, Kiowa, Blackfoot, Crow, and Shoshone. Most of the tribes visited the region on bison hunting trips. There is little evidence that the groups stayed in the area year-round. The one exception was a branch of the Shoshone known as the Sheep Eaters.

Nature's Glass

The geology of Yellowstone played an important role in American-Indian culture. Obsidian Cliff was a significant source of raw material. Obsidian is a volcanic rock that is usually dark brown to black in color. It has a glassy texture. It can hold a very sharp edge that is sharper than that of surgical steel. Obsidian was frequently used to make tools to cut meat and leather. It was also used to make spear points (left) and arrowheads. Obsidian was widely traded among Indian tribes. Tools made from obsidian originating in Obsidian Cliff have been found as far away as Ohio.

DIFFERENT LIFESTYLES

Most of the tribes that used the area that is the present-day park were nomadic hunters. They followed bison herds. They usually arrived in the Yellowstone area in late spring. They left before the first snows fell to avoid the bitter cold of winter.

One important tribe that used the area was the Blackfoot. Several Blackfoot families would join together to form bands that ranged in size from 75 to 250 individuals. The men formed the hunting parties and frequently killed several bison on a single hunting trip.

An American-Indian bison hunt is depicted in Seth Eastman's The Buffalo Hunt.

Afterward, many days were spent processing the meat. The women and children sliced the meat into thin strips that were then hung on racks to dry in the sun. Once dry, the meat was ground until it had a fine texture and then was mixed with melted bison fat, berries, and nuts and placed in rawhide sacks to harden. The Indians called this combination pemmican. It did not spoil for weeks. It was the perfect food for groups that were on the move.

The Blackfoot were almost totally dependent on bison. As a result, they often went to war with other tribes to defend their hunting grounds. Many other tribes feared the Blackfoot because they were fierce warriors and excellent horsemen.

The Gift of Life

Many American Indians believed that bison were a gift from their creator. Their lives depended on the bison—for food, clothing, tools, shelter, and fuel. The meat was eaten fresh or dried for jerky or pemmican. The tongue was considered a delicacy. The hides were used to make moccasins, shirts, dresses, belts, and tepee covers. The horns were used as cups and fire carriers. Bones were made into knives, war clubs, arrowheads, and sled runners. Bison chips (dried dung) were used as fuel for cooking, heat, and sending smoke signals. Even the tail was used as a fly swatter and for ceremonial decorations. Historians have described more than one hundred different ways that American Indians used the bison.

After European-American buffalo hunters killed off most of the large bison herds for their hides, the Blackfoot and other tribes suffered greatly. Thousands died of starvation. At the same time the U.S. government forced American-Indian groups to give up their way of life and relocate to reservations.

THE SHEEP EATERS

The Sheep Eaters were one of several groups of Shoshone Indians that lived in the region. They were called Sheep Eaters because Rocky Mountain bighorn sheep were their main food source. The Sheep Eaters lived in the higher elevations of the park, particularly in the Absaroka Mountains. They were the only group that lived in the park year-round on a regular basis.

The Sheep Eaters formed small groups of two or three families and moved frequently to find food. Only one animal was usually killed during a hunt, with the meat lasting for about a week. They would occasionally drive several sheep into traps they built, which would allow them to remain in one area longer. The Sheep Eaters also ate berries, roots, insects, birds, and small animals.

The Sheep Eaters hunted with the help of large dogs as pack animals. The families treated their dogs well, often sleeping with them. Sometimes, when a person died, his dog was buried with him so they could be together in the next life.

In the summers lodging was simple. Sometimes caves were used for shelters, and other times makeshift tepees were constructed.

The Sheep Eaters built winter dwellings called wickiups, much like this one, in Yellowstone.

In the winter the Sheep Eaters built sturdy dwellings called wicki-ups. These structures consisted of up to one hundred 10- to 18-foot (3- to 5-m) aspen poles bundled together to form a cone shape. The exteriors of wickiups were thatched with pine boughs to provide protection from cold winds and snow.

The Sheep Eaters were master craftspeople. The men boiled the large, curved horns of the bighorn sheep and straightened them into 3-foot (1-m) bows. The bows were very powerful and could drive an arrow completely through a bison. As a trade item these bows, which took up to two months to make, were in great demand. The women used animal brains to process hides into the softest and most desirable clothing possible. For added protection from the cold, they lined blankets and coats with rabbit fur.

The arrival of European Americans brought an end to the Shoshone Sheep Eaters' presence in Yellowstone. Disease carried into the area by domesticated sheep killed many of the bighorn sheep, the Sheep Eaters' major food source. Smallpox also killed many tribe members. In the early 1880s the U.S. government moved the Sheep Eaters who survived the food shortage and epidemics onto a reservation.

A New Era

The arrival of European-American fur trappers in the early 1800s resulted in a dramatic cultural change in Yellowstone. The trappers' vivid and exciting descriptions of the area captured the interest of many U.S. citizens. Soon, official expeditions were organized to explore the area. Proposals were presented to Congress to create a national park to protect the region's unique environment.

The new American culture brought to the region by tourists and trappers strongly affected Yellowstone. Control of the area slipped from the hands of the American Indians. Hunting, the major activity in the park for American Indians, was soon prohibited. The new purpose of the park was declared to be wilderness and wildlife protection and the development of tourism. The number of visitors to the park increased steadily.

Tourists explore Yellowstone during its early days as a national park.

Major construction projects were soon required to meet the needs of the increasing number of tourists. Newly paved roads allowed visitors to drive to the park's major features. Hiking paths allowed for the exploration of rustic backcountry. Service stations met travelers' needs for fuel, repairs, and other emergencies. Hotels, lodges, and campgrounds were built for lodging. Shower and laundry services were made available at various sites in the park, as were grocery stores and restaurants. Today, there are more than two thousand buildings in Yellowstone National Park. As many as 4,300 workers provide a range of services for visitors during the peak summer tourist season.

Loved to Death

Yellowstone is one of many U.S. national parks being loved to death. Automobiles clog the park's highways and emit polluting exhaust. Campgrounds are full almost every day during the peak season. In the winter, snowmobiles pierce the silence as they roar across the backcountry on guided tours. Tourists take great risks when they try to get close to large, wild animals. Americans' love for wilderness areas is posing a threat to national parks in the United States.

For several years a lack of adequate funding has posed a threat to almost all national parks, including Yellowstone National Park. Parks require more money for preservation and maintenance of roads, hiking paths, buildings, and campgrounds due to growing numbers of visitors. New education and recreation programs need to be developed. Park administrators need money to hire more rangers to patrol and protect the parks. The budget for many national parks has been cut rather than increased. Hopefully, our government leaders will soon recognize the need to properly finance and care for our national parks.

SIX

A Conflict of Opinions

Yellowstone was the first national park in the world. There was no example to look to when the decisions on how to manage it were being made. Throughout the park's history difficult issues have arisen that have required thoughtful consideration.

Determining the rights of the American Indians who had lived in the area that became the park was one of the first major issues. Many non-American Indians believed that the Indians had no rights. Some newspapers and magazines described American Indians as brutal savages who needed to be eliminated. Philetus W. Norris, the park's second superintendent (1877–1882), banned American Indians from even entering the park. This critical decision changed the environmental balance between humans and the animals living there.

MANAGING THE PARK

Another early issue was determining which federal agency should manage the park. The federal government initially gave the authority to the secretary of the interior. Nathaniel P. Langford was appointed

◀ *The challenge of protecting Yellowstone's natural surroundings and maintaining it as a national park is one of the most difficult issues facing the park today.*

Indian Unrest

In 1877 the Nez Perce were being forced off their land in the Wallowa Valley in Oregon. During a conflict with white settlers who were taking Nez Perce land, four settlers were killed. Several Nez Perce decided to flee to Canada through Yellowstone National Park. As they passed through the park, with the U.S. Army in pursuit, they came in contact with tourists. The Nez Perce took some of them as hostages. A few tourists were injured, and two were killed. This incident was used to support the claim that Indians were dangerous and therefore should be banned from the park.

as the park's first superintendent in 1872. He received no salary and only a small budget to manage the huge park. Langford, through no fault of his own, was largely ineffective.

In 1877 Philetus W. Norris became the park's second superintendent. He administered the building of the park's first roads. He also supervised the construction of the park's first headquarters, at Mammoth Springs. Although he pushed to end the American-Indian presence in the park, Norris established one of the best collections of American-Indian artifacts of the time. His appointment ended in 1882 because of political conflicts in Washington, D.C. The superintendents who followed Norris did little to develop the park.

In 1886 the secretary of the interior transferred the management of the park to the U.S. Army. Army administrators were the most effective during the park's early years. They patrolled the park for illegal activity, especially the poaching of wild animals. They were good protectors of the park's resources. However, they did little to encourage tourism.

A lasting change in park management occurred in 1916, when the National Park Service was created. The federal government designed this new agency to coordinate policies for Yellowstone and the new national parks that had been formed. The National Park Service has the power to make and enforce regulations for all national parks. These regulations carry the same authority as other federal and local laws.

Although often under-funded, the National Park Service continues to pursue two major goals in Yellowstone: to protect all living things and natural features in the park and to administer the park "For the Benefit and Enjoyment

A National Park Service ranger measures air pollutants in Yellowstone National Park.

of the People." This statement is carved on the park's Roosevelt Arch entrance.

PROTECTING THE INNOCENT

The removal and banning of American Indians from the park increased the wildlife population, especially that of bison, elk, and deer. The increased numbers of large animals attracted illegal hunters to the park. The wild animals were killed and sold for profit. Bison heads and elk antlers were in great demand in eastern markets. Newspaper photos of poachers standing with rows of bison heads enraged the public. The U.S. Congress reacted to this outrage by passing the Lacey Act

In an effort to protect Yellowstone's ▶▶ *wildlife, an act was passed in 1894. One of its measures is that fish caught in the park must be released.*

of 1894, which protects the birds, animals, and fish of Yellowstone National Park. The hunting, killing, or wounding of any bird or animal in the park is strictly prohibited. The act also provided that no fish could be caught in park waters by using seines, traps, nets, or explosives. Fish could be caught by hook and line only.

The hunting prohibition is still enforced today, with one exception. If park biologists determine that the number of animals is too great and threatens the herd's overall health, rangers can thin the herd. Fishing is permitted in restricted areas but mostly as part of a catch-and-release program.

VISITOR SAFETY

One of the main reasons tourists visit Yellowstone is to observe wild animals. Unfortunately, many visitors do not use common sense when they interact with these animals. Some individuals want to touch bears and bison as if they were in a petting zoo. This is very dangerous behavior that can lead to serious injury or death.

In the park's history at least five people have been killed by bears. Two individuals died from bison attacks. Injuries are far more common than deaths from animal attacks. Even a chipmunk can "bite the hand that feeds it." Park regulations have been created that make it illegal to feed any animal in Yellowstone National Park. Regulations also require tourists to stay at least 25 yards (23 m) away from large animals. Because bears pose the greatest risk, humans must stay at least 100 yards (91 m) from all bears.

A Change in Policy

Feeding Yellowstone's bears was a popular event for many years. Bears were allowed to search for food in the park's garbage dumps. At one time park employees even built bleachers so tourists could sit while watching bears scavenge for food in a large garbage dump. Other tourists tried to feed bears that came into their campsites. Some individuals even tried to hand food to bears from their car windows. The bears began to expect people to give them food. This situation led to tragic events. Sometimes the bears attacked without warning. Between 1931 and 1969 an average of forty-six bear attacks occurred each year in the park. In 1970 the park administrators strictly prohibited the feeding of bears. They also developed bearproof garbage dumps. Currently, bear attacks in the park are rare.

Due to the reintroduction of wolves to Yellowstone, their numbers have increased since their near extinction in the late 1800s.

THE WOLF RETURNS

By the late 1800s wolves had been hunted to near extinction in Yellowstone. They were considered dangerous animals that killed the wildlife tourists wanted to see. Local ranchers near the park disliked wolves because wolves killed their livestock. By the 1920s not a single wolf could be found in Yellowstone. Soon after, scientists began to notice ecological changes after the disappearance of the wolves. Elk populations swelled. Vegetation patterns changed. By the 1960s wildlife biologists suggested a change in policy toward the wolves.

The issue of bringing the wolves back to Yellowstone was hotly debated. Conservationists supported wolf reintroduction as a way to restore the park's original ecology. Ranchers and some hunters opposed this decision. However, in the mid-1990s, park rangers returned wolves to the park. The program has been successful, and more than ten healthy packs of wolves now roam Yellowstone.

The ecological benefits that wolves provide to the Greater Yellowstone Ecosystem have been documented. Elk enjoy eating young aspen seedlings. Without wolves as predators, the increased elk population was overgrazing on aspen sprouts. Aspen trees, which had been in decline, are now recovering in the areas where wolves hunt elk. Beaver populations are also on the rise. With the help of the wolves, the beavers do not have to compete as much with the elk for access to willow trees.

DISEASE CARRIERS

Bison management has also triggered conflict in the Yellowstone area. Almost half of all Yellowstone bison carry a disease called brucellosis. The bacterium that causes it can make pregnant female bison lose their calves. Brucellosis can be passed to domestic cattle if the cattle are exposed to infected bison. Because there are no fences around the park, bison sometimes wander across its boundaries and onto private land. This can expose ranchers' cattle to the disease.

While the likelihood of cattle contracting the disease is low, it does occur. If one of the cows in a herd contracts the disease, the entire herd must be **quarantined**. In the most serious cases, the cattle may have to be killed, causing the ranchers huge financial losses.

Park managers and ranchers are working to keep livestock and wild bison separated. They are also vaccinating cattle and bison against the disease. Cooperation between ranchers and park officials will continue to be necessary to keep brucellosis in check.

Up in Flames

Yellowstone has always had fires. While humans start some of the fires, lightning ignites most of them. Most experts believe that fires are a necessary tool for maintaining the proper ecological balance. However, some experts think that fires should be carefully controlled by humans. Park administrators enacted a policy in 1972 that

Firefighters watch the blazing flames ▶▶
during the fires of 1988.

A Record Breaker

The 1988 Yellowstone fires broke all park records. Fifty individual fires started in the park. Those fires burned across almost 36 percent of the park's surface. Firestorms killed animals, burned buildings, and even caused some fish kills. Fortunately, no humans perished in the park as a result of the fires.

allowed naturally started fires to burn themselves out without human intervention. This policy was successful in maintaining plant diversity for sixteen years.

In the summer of 1988, however, disaster struck. June and July were the driest summer months in the park in recorded history. In early July fires began to break out across the Greater Yellowstone Ecosystem. The fires were fueled by the extremely dry vegetation and spread by high winds. Flames danced across the night sky. Smoke billowed high into the air and had a smothering effect. The last hot coals of those devastating fires were finally put out in November of 1988.

The disastrous fires resulted in the creation of new fire management plans. While some natural fires are still allowed to burn themselves out, there are stricter guidelines in place for controlling fires.

SNOWMOBILES

Environmentalists and outdoor enthusiasts are engaged in a heated argument over the use of snowmobiles in the park. Winter weather brings abundant snow that creates a white wonderland. Because the heavy snows close many park roads to automobile traffic, snowmobiles are ideal for exploring the beautiful backcountry. Those who

International Distinction

Yellowstone is not only famous in the United States. It has also achieved international recognition. Yellowstone was selected as a United Nations Educational, Scientific, and Cultural Organization (UNESCO) Biosphere Reserve in 1976. It was one of the first locations in the world to be named a Biosphere Reserve. These special areas are used for studying conservation and sustainable development practices. In 1978 UNESCO also named Yellowstone National Park a World Heritage Site.

support the use of snowmobiles believe it is their right to have access to all parts of the park in the winter.

The critics of snowmobiles are just as vocal in their opposition. They believe that snowmobiles pollute the air and make an excessive amount of noise. They also think that the machines interfere with wildlife. Opponents suggest that the best and most natural way to explore the backcountry is on snowshoes or cross-country skis.

OUTSIDE DANGERS

Some scientists warn that the park is threatened by human development near its borders. One threat is the potential development of power plants that use the region's

Yellowstone National Park is one of North America's most majestic natural wonders. It is a place for many to visit and discover firsthand the power of nature.

geothermal and other energy resources. A second danger is mining activity and the pollution it causes.

Geothermal energy plants use the earth's internal heat to produce electricity. Much of the Yellowstone area sits on a hot spot that is close to the land surface. Geothermal plants can use heat to produce electricity without creating air pollution. However, opponents fear that tapping into that natural heat energy could interfere with the thermal features (geysers, fumaroles, and hot springs) in the park. The National Park Service has recommended a ban on all geothermal plant development within a 15-mile (24-km) radius of Yellowstone National Park.

Gold and silver mining took place in the past within 5 miles (8 km) of the park's boundary. Toxic mining wastes from fifty to seventy years ago can still be found in Soda Butte Creek's drainage basin. Soda Butte Creek flows into the park and could carry these harmful wastes into the park's waters if not properly monitored.

In the 1990s a large gold, silver, and copper mine was scheduled to open just outside the park. To protect the park from potential danger, the federal government traded some of its assets for the mine property. The land is now under the watchful eye of the U.S. Forest Service.

A Crown Jewel

Yellowstone National Park is an important symbol to the people of the United States. The park represents the grandness and beauty of nature.

No similar place exists in the world, and the park must be protected.

An effective way to protect the park would be to ban all humans from entering it. With its popularity among tourists, that is not likely to happen. The best way to protect Yellowstone, while allowing people to enjoy its wonders and beauty has been debated since the creation of the park. The same debate will continue into the future. The decisions are likely to change as Americans continue to review their relationship with nature.

Glossary

aneroid barometer   an instrument used to measure air pressure

anthropologist   a person who studies the physical, cultural, and social characteristics of humans

caldera   a large depression created by a volcanic explosion or the collapse of a volcanic cone

continental divide   the natural line of mountain summits that separate waters that flow toward the Atlantic Ocean from those that flow toward the Pacific Ocean

ecosystem   all the living and nonliving things in a defined area; soil, water, plants, and animals are all part of an ecosystem

hydrogen sulfide   a colorless, flammable, poisonous gas composed of two parts hydrogen and one part sulfur, which smells like rotten eggs

magma   melted rock that is located below the crust of the earth

quarantine   the practice of keeping a person or animal away from others to stop the spread of disease

sulfuric acid   a liquid that is capable of dissolving rock and is composed of two parts hydrogen, one part sulfur, and four parts oxygen

swarm   a great number of earthquakes that occur in a short period of time

ungulates   mammals that have hooves

volcanism   volcanic force or activity

Fast Facts

Name: Yellowstone National Park

Date established: March 1, 1872

Location: Northwestern Wyoming, southwestern Montana, southeastern Idaho

Size: 3,472 square miles (8,992 sq km)

Geothermal features: More than 10,000 geothermal features, including hot springs, mud pots, fumaroles, and geysers

Waterfalls: More than three hundred

Rivers: Yellowstone, Madison, Lamar, Bechler, Lewis

Animals: Elk, bison, deer, moose, American pronghorn, wolves, bears, beavers, Rocky Mountain bighorn sheep, bald eagles, sandhill cranes, trumpeter swans

Plants: Douglas fir, lodgepole pine, aspen, willow, Ross's bentgrass, sand verbena, death camas, water hemlock

Major expeditions: Folsom Party, Washburn-Doane Expedition, Hayden and Barlow parties

American Indians: Twenty-six American-Indian tribes used the park region, including the Sioux, Comanche, Crow, Blackfoot, Kiowa, and Shoshone Sheep Eaters

American pronghorn

Number of tourists: Almost 3 million each year

National Historic Landmarks: Fort Yellowstone; Norris, Madison, and Fishing Bridge Museums; Obsidian Cliff; Old Faithful Inn; Northeast Entrance Station

International recognition: UNESCO Biosphere Reserve, UNESCO World Heritage Site

Management issues: Feeding of animals, reintroduction of wolves, control of bison diseases, control of fires, use of snowmobiles

Environmental threats: Automobile traffic, poaching, mining, and geothermal plant development near the park's borders

Find Out More

BOOKS

Apel, Melanie Ann. *The Yellowstone Park Fire of 1988.* New York: Rosen Publishing Group, 2004.

Aretha, David. *Yellowstone National Park: Adventure, Explore, Discover.* Berkeley Heights, NJ: Enslow, 2008.

Rubin, Ken. *Volcanoes & Earthquakes.* New York: Simon & Schuster Children's Publishing, 2007.

DVDS

The Wildlife of Yellowstone. West Yellowstone: Yellowstone Media Group, 2007.

The Wonders of Yellowstone. West Yellowstone: Yellowstone Media Group, 2007.

WEB SITES

Inside Yellowstone
www.nps.gov/archive/yell/insideyellowstone/index.htm
A high-interest series of educational videos narrated by Yellowstone National Park rangers.

Mountain Visions: Yellowstone National Park
http://mountainvisions.com/QTVR/YellQTVR/YellQTVR.html
Displays 360-degree panoramas of special locations in Yellowstone National Park with sound tracks.

Windows into Wonderland
http://windowsintowonderland.org
Offers informative virtual field trips exploring various aspects of Yellowstone National Park.

Yellowstone National Park Pictures
www.terragalleria.com/parks/np.yellowstone.html
Features stunning photos of several sites with diverse natural features.

Index

Page numbers in **boldface** are illustrations and charts.

Absaroka Mountain Range, 11, 20, 23
American Indians
    Blackfoot, 49, 63–65
    creation story, 61
    Crow, 48
    effect of European-Americans, 67, 71, 72–73, 74
    family and tribal groups, 60–62
    first inhabitants, 47–48
    Kiowa, **47**, 48
    language, 61
    Nez Perce, 72
    pemmican, 64
    religion/spirituality, 61
    respect for land, 59–60
    Sheep Eaters, 65–67
    Shoshone, **58**, 65–67
    tribes/groups, 62
    wickiups, 66, **66**
animal life, 29–41, 76, 77, 78–80
antelope, 33
Atlantic Ocean, 23

bald eagle, **36**, 36–37
Baronett, John, 53
bears, 39, **39**, 77, **77**
beavers, 39–41, **40**, 79
Bechler River, 23
bighorn sheep, 33–34, **34**, 65–67
Biosphere Reserve, 83
birds, 35–38

bison, **32**, 32–33, 63–65, 76, 79–80
brucellosis, 79–80
buffalo, **32**, 32–33, 63–65, 76, 79–80
The Buffalo Hunt (Eastman), **63**

caldera, 13, 20, 24
carnivores, 30
cattle, 79–80
Clark, William, 48
climate, 25, 27
Colter, John, 8, 48, 49, 50
Columbia River, 23
construction projects, 68–69
continental divide, 23
Cook, Charles, 51
Cooke, Jay, 57

death camas, 45, **45**
Doane, Gustavus C., 51–52

Eagle Peak, 11
earthquakes, 7, 19–20
ecology, 78–79, 80, 82–83
ecosystem, 13, 29
elk, 31, **31**, 78–79
environmental concerns, 69, 78–79, 83–86
Everts, Truman C., 53
exploration, 48–55

federal management, 56
fires, 80, **81**, 82–83
fishing, **75**, 76
Folsom, David, 51
Folsom Party, 51
Fort Yellowstone, 9
fumaroles, 16, **17**
fur trapping, 48, 50, 67

geography
    borders/boundaries, 5–6, 11,
        29
    elevation, 11
    landmass, 5–6
    rivers and lakes, 23
    size, 5–6
geothermal activity, 7, 8, 13–17, 18
geothermal energy plants, 86
geysers, 16–17, **18**
glaciers, 7
Grand Canyon of the Yellowstone,
    23
The Grand Canyon of the Yellowstone
    (Moran), 55, **55**
Grant, Ulysses S., 5
grassland meadows, 42–43
Greater Yellowstone Ecosystem,
    29, 79, 82
Guld of Mexico, 23

Hayden, Ferdinand V., 52, 54–55,
    56
Hayden and Barlow Parties, 52,
    54–55
Hayden Valley, 44

herbivores, 30
hot springs, 14, **15**, 16
human activity, 7–9
hunting, 73, 74, 76

Ice Age, 20–21

Jackson, William, 56

Lacey Act, 74–76
lakes, 23
Lake Yellowstone. *See* Yellowstone
    Lake
Lamar Valley, 44
Langford, Nathaniel P., 51–52, 55,
    56, 57, 71–72
Lewis and Clark Expedition, 8, 48
Lewis River, 23
lizards, 41
lodgepole pines, 42, **43**
Lower Falls, 21, **21**

Mammoth Springs, **26**–27
management of Yellowstone, 56,
    71–74
maps
    geopolitical, **6**
    physical, **12**
Midway Geyser Basin, **10**
Minerva Springs, **28**
mining, 86
Missouri River, 23
moose, 33
Moran, Thomas, 55, 57
mud pots, 16

National Historic Landmarks, 9
National Park Service, 5, 73–74
National Park Service employees, 9
Norris, Madison, and Fishing Bridge Museums, 9
Norris, Philetus W., 71, 72
Northeast Entrance Station, 9
Northern Pacific Railroad, 57

obsidian, 62, **62**
Obsidian Cliff, 9, 62
Old Faithful, 17, **18**
Old Faithful Inn, 9
omnivores, 30

Pacific Ocean, 23
Peterson, WIlliam, 51
plant life, 42, 44–45, 78–79
poaching, 73, 74, 76
pollution, 69, 86
Potts, John, 49
power plants, 84, 86
predators, 34–37
Pritchett, George, 53
pronghorn, 33
protecting Yellowstone, 9

rattlesnake, 41
reptiles, 41
Richter scale, 19
river otters, 35
rivers, 23
Rocky Mountains, 25
Ross's bentgrass, 44

safety of visitors, 76, 77
sandhill crane, 37–38, **38**
Scribner's Monthly, 53, 55
seasons, 25, 27
seismograph, 19
Smithsonian American Art Museum, 55
Snake River, 23
snakes, 41
snowmobiles, 83–84
Soda Butte Creek, 86
Steamboat Geyser, 19
supervolcano, 13–14
swarms, 20

"Thirty-Seven Days of Peril," 53
tourism, 8–9, 25, 27, 67–69, 73, 76, 77
trumpeter swan, 374

U. S. Capitol, 55
U. S. National Park Service. *See* National Park Service
United Nations Educational, Scientific, and Cultural Organization (UNESCO), 83
Upper Falls, 21

volcanic activity, 7, 13–14, 19

Washburn, Henry D., 51–52, **52**
Washburn-Doane Expedition, 17, 51–52
waterfalls, 20–21, **21**, 23
water hemlock, 45

weather, 25, 27
wildlife, 29–41, 76, 77, 78–80
wolf, **78**, 78–79
wolves, 34–35, **35**
World Heritage Site, 83

Yellowstone Lake, 24, **24**
Yellowstone National Park
    construction projects, 68–69
    creation of, 56–57
    management of, 56, 71–74
    name origin, 7
    protection of, 9
    removal and banning of America
        Indians, 71, 72–74, 74
    visitor safety, 76, 77
Yellowstone River, **22**, 23
Yellowstone sand verbena, 44

ABOUT THE AUTHORS

Byron Augustin is a nationally known Regents' Professor of Geography at Texas State University. His love for geography has led to his passion for traveling. He has visited forty-nine of the fifty United States, twenty-six of Mexico's thirty-one states, and eight Canadian provinces. Augustin has also visited fifty-five countries on five of the seven continents.

Augustin has written books, chapters, and articles in refereed scholarly journals. For Marshall Cavendish he wrote Nature's Wonders, *The Grand Canyon* and Cultures of the World, *Andorra*. He is also a professional photographer. More than twelve hundred of his photos have been published worldwide.

Jake Kubena teaches geography, Spanish, and martial arts in Wimberley, Texas. He earned a Bachelor of Science degree and a Masters of Applied Geography degree from Texas State University. Kubena has edited many geography books and enjoys traveling. He has traveled extensively in the United States and Europe.